WHY SHOULD I HELP?

BARRON'S

Books in the
WHY SHOULD I? Series:

WHY SHOULD I Protect Nature?   WHY SHOULD I Eat Well?
WHY SHOULD I Recycle?   WHY SHOULD I Help?
WHY SHOULD I Save Water?   WHY SHOULD I Listen?
WHY SHOULD I Save Energy?   WHY SHOULD I Share?

First edition for the United States, its territories and dependencies,
and Canada published in 2005 by Barron's Educational Series, Inc.

First published in Great Britain in 2001 by Hodder Wayland, an
imprint of Hodder Children's Books.
© Copyright 2001 Hodder Wayland
Hodder Children's Books
A division of Hodder Headline Ltd.
338 Euston Road
London NW1 3BH
United Kingdom
Reprinted 2002 and 2004

All inquiries should be addressed to:
Barron's Educational Series, Inc.
250 Wireless Boulevard
Hauppauge, NY 11788
www.barronseduc.com

International Standard Book Number 0-7641-3218-0

Library of Congress Catalog Card Number 2004113860

Printed in China
9 8 7 6 5 4 3 2 1

WHY SHOULD I HELP?

Written by Claire Llewellyn

Illustrated by Mike Gordon

BARRON'S

Every morning, at my house,
there are jobs to be done.

Making the beds ...

feeding the pets ...

and clearing away
the breakfast dishes.

5

And there are more jobs
to do in the evening.
Setting the table ...

doing the dishes ...

and helping to run
the bath for Charlie.

Sometimes I don't feel like helping.
I want to do something else instead.
Like finish a drawing …

watch TV ...

Would you take this coffee up to Dad for me?

Why should I help other people?
No one ever helps me!

Dad said, "Everyone needs a helping hand now and then. Remember what happened when you fell off your bike?"

"That nice boy helped you back home."

"And what happened when you forgot your costume at last year's Christmas party?"

"Mom rode home during her lunch hour to get it."

"And do you remember what happened that day you lost Squeaky?"

Ahhh, Squeaky's gone!

"Ben, Grandpa, Grandma, and I searched for him the whole afternoon."

It was all true.
I did sometimes need
a helping hand.
And I suppose other people
need one, too.

When they're busy ...

or tired …

or just a bit slow.

I'll get it!

People help one another all the time.

So I'm going to help people, too.
Helping people makes me feel grown-up,
and gives me a good feeling inside.

23

And sometimes, just sometimes, there's an extra bonus for helping. Like the time I went shopping for my Grandma ...

and she had extra time to make some pancakes.

And because I fed the fish
for Ben ...

he brought me back a present from his vacation.

All sorts of people need
help out there,
so give someone
a helping hand.

Who knows?
The next person
to need help
might be you!

Notes for parents and teachers

Why Should I?

These books will help young readers to recognize what they like and dislike, what is fair and unfair, and what is right and wrong; to think about themselves, learn from their experiences, and recognize what they are good at. Some titles in this series will help to teach children how to make simple choices that improve their health and well-being, to maintain personal hygiene, and to learn rules for, and ways of, keeping safe, including basic road safety. Reading these books will help children recognize how their behavior affects other people, to listen to other people, play and work cooperatively, and that family and friends should care for one another.

About *Why Should I Help?*

Why Should I Help? is intended to be an enjoyable book that discusses the importance of helping other people. A variety of situations throughout this book explore the value of helping children move in different worlds – in the family, their schools, and their neighborhood. Helping other people encourages children to become active members of their communities. Communities are built by people helping one another and making a contribution. Taking an active part in family life prepares children for becoming active members of society.

Helping other people is a way of forming and strengthening relationships. It is important that children see and understand how family members care

30

for one another. Lending a hand to set the table, play with the baby, or feed the rabbit are a recognition of the give-and-take nature of family life.

Helping at home or at school is one of the ways in which children begin to take responsibility for themselves. Hanging up their clothes or cleaning up the classroom are signs that children are moving from dependency toward independence and responsibility.

Recognizing when people need help is an important step in learning about other people's feelings. Children need to become aware of the needs of other people, whatever their age. Of course, it is vital that children are thanked for their help. Positive feedback makes children feel good about themselves and enhances their self-esteem.

Suggestions as you read the book with children

As you read this book with children, stop occasionally to discuss the issues raised in the text. Do they have jobs to do around the house? How do they feel about this? Think about all the jobs their moms or dads do. Do their parents enjoy doing these jobs? Are there some jobs they really hate?

Look at the examples given in the text of when Suzy needed help. Has something similar ever happened to them? Was somebody there to help them?

There is a police officer in this book. Police officers are just some of the people in uniform who are there to help us. Can they think of any others? Why is a uniform so useful? Can they imagine a time when they might need to seek help for themselves?

Suggested follow-up activities

Plan a group task, such as making a model, which might entail helping fellow students or friends.

Ask the children to draw up a list of things they can do by themselves and things for which they need help. Why are there some things they can do alone and other things they can't?

What words, phrases, or sayings can they think of that have to do with helping? What do people mean when they say the following?

Many hands make light work   Help yourself
Too many cooks spoil the broth   Helpline
Lend a hand   Helpmate
Every little bit helps   First aid

Books to read

Digby Helps at the Zoo by Alan Aburrow-Newman and Gill Guile (Brimax Books, 1996)

Franklin Helps Out by Paulette Bourgeois (Kids Can Press, 2000)

Honey Helps by Laura Godwin (Perfection Learning Prebound, 2001)